KEYS TO BECOMING AN EFFECTIVE WORSHIP LEADER

by Tom Kraeuter

TRAINING RESOURCES

8929 Old LeMay Ferry Rd • Hillsboro, MO 63050 • (314) 789-4522

Keys to Becoming an Effective Worship Leader
by Tom Kraeuter

Unless otherwise identified, Scripture quotations are from either the King Kames Version or the New American Standard Bible, copyright The Lockman Foundation 1960, 1961, 1962, 1963, 1968, 1971, 1972, 1973, 1975, 1977. Used by permission.

Cover design by: Steve Barker, Nashville, TN
Cover illustration by: David Wariner, Corydon, IN

Dedication

I gratefully dedicate this book to Dave Lorenz, the man who discipled me in worship leading and taught me much about simply being a worshipper of God. Thanks, Dave, for your sensitivity to the Holy Spirit, your amazing patience, and your unending dedication to the Lord. I learned more from you than you can imagine!

Thanks to

- *The worship team of Christian Outreach Church in Hillsboro, Missouri for being so patient with me while I've learned the lessons which I am sharing in this book.*

- *Those from whom I have learned so much about worship, especially Nick Ittzes and Kent Henry*

- *Jennifer Waggoner for her fine copy editing*

- *Diane Lopez for her meticulous proofreading*

- *Michael Ostermann and Diana Longwell for reviewing this manuscript from the worship leader's perspective*

And special thanks to my wife, Barbara, who has been my constant encourager.

Contents

Introduction

ef-fect'-ive *adj.* producing a definite or desired result, efficient

As a worship leader I have a long-term goal: to consistently lead the people before the throne of God that they might commune with Him. That is my "desired result." I desire to do it as well and as efficiently as possible.

When I began leading worship I was quite naive. I felt that if I simply worshipped, everyone would follow. Although to some degree this is true, I have found that there is more to it than this alone.

Some time ago someone asked me what it was that made me effective as a worship leader. I thought for a moment and then responded, "Well, if you've got a couple hours I could give you some of the basics." That conversation was the beginning of this book. In over twelve years of leading worship the Lord has allowed me to learn some powerful keys to being effective in this ministry.

Please note that this book is not entitled "How to Lead Worship." In fact I have included very few keys regarding the practice of actual leading. This is more a book on *being* a worship leader: the practical everyday-ness of the position itself.

This book is also not meant to be all-inclusive. I honestly do not consider myself an authority on the subject. I have merely been in the right place at the right time and have been privileged to learn some key principles as time went by. Because Scripture does not speak directly to most of the practical areas of being a worship leader much of this book is based on experience using Scriptural concepts as a foundation. Some of the truths in this book were learned through struggles, some by trial and error and others have been picked up from those who have walked before me in these things. Regardless, all are valuable lessons which, if applied, can potentially save the reader much heartache, time and energy.

If you are the main worship leader at a church this information will prove invaluable. On the other hand, if you only occasionally lead worship for a home Bible study you can still benefit immensely from this material. You will merely need to make application to your particular situation. For example, the section on "Caring for the Congregation" should be understood to mean whatever "congregation" you are serving, whether it is five people or 5,000.

Obviously not everything in this book will apply to

every situation. These are meant to be guidelines to becoming a more effective worship leader. My overall recommendation for using this book is to read only one chapter at a time. The chapters are purposely short to allow for quick reading. When you finish a chapter, prayerfully consider what the Lord would have you do with the information you have just read. Then begin to implement the things you feel are applicable to your situation.

My prayer for you is that the Lord would abundantly bless your work and ministry for Him. ❖

Chapter 1

Maintaining a Strong Relationship With the Lord

Some time ago I heard an elderly gentleman discussing how his priorities had changed over the years. As a youth he had been taught that certain things were important. Over time he had abandoned many of those values and embraced new ideals. But as he grew in years and wisdom, he found himself doing another reversal. Those things which he had left behind were once again becoming top priority. He had realized that the standards he had learned as a youngster really contained lasting value.

I have gone through much the same process in my years of leading worship. I first began leading worship mostly out of a deep, intense gratitude to the Lord. He had redeemed me! He had, as the psalmist said, "brought me up out of the pit of destruction, out of the miry clay; and He set my feet upon a rock making my footsteps firm" (Psalm 40:2). I wanted to verbalize my appreciation. Beyond saving me, He had become my friend and constant companion. To this day I still have trouble grasping that the almighty God of all creation would desire *me*. But I had accepted the truth of His Word and my heart was filled with unending gratitude toward God.

From the beginning of my walk with the Lord it was obvious to me and others that He had called me to leadership. Therefore, it was only natural that my gratitude would spill over onto others and I would end up leading others into this same expression of appreciation, or worship. But the expression itself was more important to me than leading others in it. I just wanted to love and honor God.

As time went on, however, I began to realize that other dynamics played into the worship leading process. My musical abilities and understanding became increasingly important. I looked at the type and style of music being used and its affect on the song-service. I began to grasp how people's relationships affected their worship. Even the other musicians and their abilities came to play a more important role in my understanding of how worship "works." I began more and more to take my cues from people's reactions to the "worship" instead of from the Lord. I had almost completely abandoned the once simple gratitude-based relationship I had with God. Concepts effecting worship leading had become my focus more than the Lord Himself. I was more in touch with the process than I was with God. I was not spending time with the Lord developing our relationship. In fact, the only real quality time I was spending with God was while I was leading.

At first I was able to fool most of the people while I went through the above scenario, due at least in part, to the strong gifts which God had given me. No one really knew that I was more conscious of the techniques than I was of the Lord. Still, as time went on, my drifting from God became more obvious and had the potential for getting much worse.

I had reached bottom. I was not leading worship from a heart full of worship; I was leading using techniques alone. The tools which God had provided to be effective in leading *worship* had become an end in themselves. The reactions of people had become more important to me than having a heart which desired to please God. I was not really leading worship. In reality I was only toying with people's emotions, including my own.

Fortunately, I once more experienced the rescuing, redeeming power of the Lord. His unending mercies touched me where I needed them most and I saw the falsehood of what I was doing. By His grace I was able to recognize that the path I was on was quite a distance from the one I should have been on. The Lord graciously brought me back into that simple grateful relationship we had before. There were no lightning bolts from heaven or earth-shaking revelations, just a simple understanding of His new-every-morning mercies. I could once again lead worship out of a heart which radiated true worship.

In going through this process I learned some lasting principles. The most obvious was this: the only way to be effective long-term as a worship leader is to maintain a close relationship with the Lord.

If I am not in constant pursuit of a close relationship with the Lord, if I am not continually allowing Him to fill this empty vessel, then I will have nothing to give. I may have some nifty tricks that will "pull me through a few services" but beyond that, I'm empty. I need to be daily renewed and refreshed by Jesus, the living water. If I forego this ongoing relationship with Him, I have really missed the fullness of His calling on my life.

Anyone aspiring to be an effective worship leader must have as their main anchor point maintaining a relationship with the object of their worship, the almighty God. Throughout this book I will discuss other ideas and concepts to help you on your path to becoming the most effective leader of worship you can be. However, maintaining your relationship with the Lord is foundational to it all. You would not expect to be a close friend of a person with whom you never spend time. Relationships take time, and lots of it, to develop. In the same way, it is essential to spend time with the Lord, just as you would spend time cultivating an earthly friendship. Nothing — absolutely nothing — is more important. ❖

Chapter 2

Having a Humble, Servant Attitude

The ultimate musician in late twentieth century America is one who spends nearly his entire life studying music and usually a specific instrument. His course is fixed on one singular purpose — "to make it to the top." Good is not good enough. He must be the very best or he is a complete and utter failure. He will use and abuse people to accomplish his goals. If his talents and training are of a high enough caliber, and if he gets to know the right people, he will ultimately be rewarded with the opportunity to regularly perform before hundreds, thousands, and even before the leaders of society. The ultimate worshipper in approximately 1000 B.C. Israel spends his time guarding the family's sheep and making up songs about the faithful God he serves. He apparently has no aspirations toward anything more and is quite content in what he is doing. If no one ever sees or recognizes his talents he is satisfied to worship and serve the Lord. His reward is to intimately know God and to know that God Himself will protect and provide for him. Although it was never his aim, he ultimately finds that his musical gifts, which he has diligently cultivated before the Lord, make a way for him to stand before the ruler of the nation.

Is it not amazing how different the modern philosophy of success is than David's? The difference is probably even more significant when you realize that the Bible refers to David as "a man after God's own heart" (I Samuel 13:14). If David's attitude really reflects the heart of God then what does this other attitude reflect?

In Psalm 51:17, David writes "The sacrifices of God are a broken spirit; a broken and a contrite heart, O God, Thou wilt not despise." It was with great trepidation that one day I realized these words, "broken" and "contrite" characterize the hearts and lives of very few musicians today... even in the church. It seems that "making the big-time" is "where it's at." Even "making it big for God" is often-used terminology.

Ultimately, though, the Lord doesn't need our talents — He wants our hearts. All the abilities we can muster are of very little eternal consequence. God is looking for a broken and contrite heart, one that is not self-centered but focused on Him.

Long before Jesus was ever born, David understood the concept of being a servant and being faithful in the little things (Luke 19:17). He simply did what was put before him knowing that God was the One who held the future. If promotion was to come it would come by His hand, not by David's attempting to manipulate the circumstances. Even after Samuel anointed him as king, David refused to take matters into his own hands. Instead, he chose to allow the Lord to move sovereignly on his behalf. How contradictory to our normal ways!

Jesus told us that He did not come to be served but to serve. He taught that His followers should do as He did. "If any man desire to be first, the same shall be last of all, and servant of all" (Mark 9:35). Again, how contrary this is to our society's view of success. We do not really understand what it means to be a servant. We need to pray that God will reveal how we can manifest this servant attitude within our lives.

In practical terms, we can be a servant in many ways. We can serve the Lord by worshipping and obeying Him in all that we do and say. We can serve our church by constantly learning and growing in the things which will enable us to better lead others in worship. We can serve our pastor by honoring him with our words and our actions. We can daily decide that in all we do and say we will, like Jesus and like David, be humble servants. ❖

Chapter 3

Having a Levitical Heart

"**T**hus shalt thou separate the Levites from among the children of Israel: and the Levites shall be mine. And after that shall the Levites go in to do the service of the tabernacle of the congregation: and thou shalt cleanse them, and offer them for an offering. For they are wholly given unto me from among the children of Israel..." (Numbers 8:14-16).

Without question the Levites' main purpose was simply

to be given unto God. They were an offering, as it were, unto Him. Anything else in their lives was of secondary importance. All that they did and said was consecrated unto God. Nothing outweighed their belonging to Him.

Obviously, we are not Levites in the literal sense because we are not direct descendants from the tribe of Levi. However, even beyond the clear musical similarities, there seems to be a strong correlation between what God required of the Levites and what He requires of those of us involved in the ministry of praise and worship. He is not just looking for talented musicians. He wants our hearts. Our main purpose in life is simply to *be* to His glory.

Ephesians 1:12 tells us that as believers we are to *"be* to the praise of His glory."* How much more is this true for worship leaders. We, as worship leaders, should model for others this idea of existing for God's glory, and yet we too often get so busy with the things of God that we miss simply *being* to the praise of His glory. The Lord isn't nearly as interested in our abilities as He is interested in us. The very essence of our existence is not to *do* but to *be* to His glory.

The opening Scripture passage in this chapter clearly states that the Levites were "given wholly" to God. I Chronicles 16:4-6 tells us that the Levites were regularly before the Lord. It wasn't a once-in-a-while thing for them; this was their life.

This attitude of being given completely to the Lord needs to permeate our lives also. Some years ago my wife and I decided to build a house. At the time, I was the bass player on the worship team at the church where I now lead worship. This was obviously not a full-time or even part-time position. My full-time occupation was in sales for a company located 40 miles from our church.

In choosing a location to build our house, we considered many factors. Anyone who has ever moved into a new home can relate. We considered how far it was to work, to schools, shopping and major highways. We discussed utilities, garbage pickup, zoning restrictions, etc., etc., etc. All of these were important and needed to be considered. Ultimately, however, one factor proved to be decisive: the proximity to our church. Even though I was at church only two or three times per week, and even though I was only the bass player, God had put within me this Levitical heart attitude. I realized that my main reason for being was to be given totally to the Lord. This meant that my first priority was Him and what He had called me to. Everything else, including the daily 80-mile round trip for work, paled in comparison.

It is important to mention that I did not do this to get something from God. My motivation was that I simply wanted to honor Him with my life, regardless of the consequences.

I share this story, not in hopes that you will think I am a great guy, but to stir all of us more toward the daily attitude of being given to God. All the abilities that I possess, all the talents I can claim are, in the final analysis, of very little importance to God. He wants my life. Without that, He cannot even begin to use the other things to their full potential.

Our giving ourselves unto Him must be without any conditions. Too often we say or think something like this, "God, I will be totally Yours if You will let me be important, if You will let people esteem me." The Lord has no use for our restrictions. He requires our lives.

The bottom line is this: we must decide that if God never uses us in any "big" way that we will still be His. We are to *be* to the praise of *His* glory, regardless of circumstances or situations. No restrictions, no hidden clauses. We are His... Levites, given totally to Him. ❖

Chapter 4

Living a Life of Worship

I am convinced that we will never fully enter into worship as God desires us to until we learn to live out a lifestyle of praise and worship. We need to teach this concept to our congregations, but more importantly, we as worship leaders must live it. I have heard it said that the worship of the sanctuary is meaningless unless it is preceded by six days of worship as a way of life. If we really understand and walk in the grace of God this statement is a bit strong. Nevertheless, it has merit. We cannot go out and live in a manner contrary to what the Lord wants for us and then come in on Sunday morning and expect to fully worship God. It simply does not work. In reality, our Sunday morning experience of worship should be the by-product of an entire week of worship unto the Lord.

I find it very interesting to note that John 4:23 tells us that God is seeking worshippers. It does not say He is looking for worship but worship*pers*. Occasional worship is not enough. The Lord desires people who emanate worship, people who live worship — worshippers.

I love the story in Acts 16 about Paul and Silas in prison. Verses 22 through 24 tell us that they had their clothes torn off of them, were beaten, were thrown into prison and were fastened in stocks. Once when I read this account, I wondered what I would have done in that situation. It says that Paul and Silas "prayed and sang praises to God." My immediate reaction was, "Lord, if I was confronted with a situation that extreme, would I react like that?" I was not sure.

Several years ago I read a number of books talking about the need to praise God in difficult circumstances. I recall that they discussed the necessity of doing this, but I do not remember any of them telling *how* to do it. Praising the Lord in a crisis situation is not a natural response for us. When we find ourselves in any type of crisis we will react in one of two ways. We will either panic or we will respond out of that which has been built within us. Paramedics, for example, when confronted with a serious automobile accident are prepared for the situation. They do not panic because this is what they have been trained for. It should be the same way with us. If we cultivate praise and worship into our everyday lives, we will have the proper response when we find ourselves in a crisis circumstance — worshipping God. But this will only happen if we build the daily-ness of praise and worship into our lives.

The Bible exhorts us again and again that our praise and worship is to be ongoing. "I will bless the Lord *at all times*" (Psalm 34:1). "From the rising of the sun to its setting the name of the Lord is to be praised" (Psalm 113:3). "Through Him then, let us *continually* offer up a sacrifice of praise to God, that is, the fruit of lips that give thanks to His name" (Hebrews 13:15).

We must realize that worshiping God really is our reason for existing. "But you are a chosen race, a royal priesthood, a holy nation, a people for God's own possession, *that you may proclaim the excellencies of Him* who has called you out of darkness into His marvelous light" (I Peter 2:9). We were made and redeemed for the purpose of proclaiming His excellencies. This is not just singing songs. If God wanted music we could just play a tape for Him. He is not ultimately interested in music per se; He wants our lives. The Lord is looking for lives which proclaim His excellencies, lives which are completely given to Him and His purposes, lives of worship unto Him.

This life of worship must permeate everything we do and say. Mother Theresa was once asked what worship meant to her. Without hesitation she said that Jesus had told us how to bless the Lord: "'In as much as you have done it unto the least of these, my brethren, you have done it unto Me.' Find the least," she said, "and treat them as you would treat the Lord." If we were to regularly start our day with a simple, sincere prayer like, "Lord, be glorified in all that I do and say today," would it influence our lifestyle and ultimately our corporate worship? Undoubtedly.

If we will grasp and walk in this concept there will be an automatic difference in our corporate worship gatherings. Consider the following scenario for a moment: you and everyone within your congregation live a life of worship from Monday through Saturday. The heart attitude of everyone involved is to be given unto God and to His purposes. Daily there are songs of praise going forth, acts of kindness toward a hurting world, hearts communing with the Lord. Then, on Sunday morning, everyone comes together to worship the Lord corporately. In doing so, their worship becomes simply an overflow of what they had been doing in their daily lives for the last six days. Do you suppose that the corporate worship experience would be any different than that to which you are accustomed? Of course it would! It would not necessarily be more acceptable to God because we have been "good," for only the blood of Jesus makes us acceptable. But the entire attitude and atmosphere would be changed to match God's heart for our worship.

God desires us to continually have an attitude of worship in all that we do and say. This, in turn, will enhance our corporate worship. ❖

Chapter 5

Thankfulness Unto God

My son's earliest understanding of prayer was simply saying "Thank you" to God. I purposely endeavored to instill this in him. Yes, I want him to have the confidence in the Lord to be able to make requests and petitions, but it was a higher priority for me to train him to be thankful. We live in a very thankless society. I am constantly amazed at the reactions of store clerks, waiters/waitresses, gas station attendants and others when I tell them thanks for whatever service or help they have just rendered. Often it seems as though no one has ever given them thanks before. They are not certain how to respond to those simple words, "Thank you."

I am convinced that we as Christians should be models of thankfulness. We should cultivate thankfulness in our everyday interactions with people. More importantly, however, we need to cultivate continual thankfulness toward God. I already mentioned that when I met the Lord I needed to be rescued. I needed more than simple consoling. I needed the forgiveness that only Jesus could provide for I was like the prostitute in Scripture whose sins were so great. Jesus explained to the people that the reason her love for Him was so great was because she had been forgiven of so much (Luke 7:37-50). I have been forgiven of all the sins I have ever committed (and they are many). As a result I have much love in my heart for my Redeemer.

He not only forgave me when I "got saved," but His forgiveness and tender mercies are new every morning (Lamentations 3:23). Although I was (and am) far from deserving, He continually showers me with His grace. No matter where I go, God is with me (Psalm 139:7-10). Even going beyond forgiveness and His constant companionship, God has now made me His son. "Behold, what manner of love the Father hath bestowed upon us, that we should be called the sons of God..." (I John 3:1). With a realization of such great love, how could I not have a heart which overflows with thanksgiving?

Meditating upon and understanding the Lord's marvelous love for us will help make us a thankful people. However, for many this alone is often not enough. Sometimes we need to do as Hebrews 13:15 tells us to do: "...let us continually *offer up a sacrifice of praise* to God..." It is not always easy to be thankful, but it is always necessary. Sometimes we need to offer a sacrifice of praise.

There are also other practical steps we can take to help cultivate thankfulness. One of the main ones is to simply make thanking God a habit.

When the children of Israel were led out of Egypt they were thankful... for a while. They were elated that their God had rescued them from their slavery. Then, slowly, the old habits they had learned under their harsh taskmasters resurfaced. The complaining and bickering had been deeply ingrained in them over many years of slavery. The simple realization that God had saved them from their terrible predicament was no longer enough.

Unfortunately, Israel missed the concept of making thanksgiving a daily habit. They did not see the importance of replacing their complaining attitude with hearts full of thanksgiving. But we can learn from their errors. If we can learn to be thankful in whatever situation we find ourselves, we will be well on our way toward living the lives that God wants us to live.

Daily make giving thanks to the Lord a habit in your own life. Mentally stop yourself from complaining or even being complacent. Instead, give thanks to God. A heart that is daily full of thanksgiving to the Lord will be much more effective in leading corporate worship. ❖

Chapter 6

Walking in God's Grace

"How can I lead worship? I have failed God over and over again. I even know better and I still blow it. He could not possibly use *me* to bring people into His presence, could He?" I cannot begin to tell you the number of times I have heard these thoughts from people involved in the ministry of praise and worship. It has probably been on the lips of, or, at the very least, on the mind of everyone who has ever aspired to lead God's people in worship. Every one of us at some point in time has felt as though we have failed the Lord by our actions or words.

Of all the problems within the church today, I believe that the most prevalent is a failure to comprehend or fully believe the power of the gospel of Jesus. As I travel and talk with people, the thing they seem to despise the most is their own consistent inadequacies and failures before the Lord. There is no question that we have failed the Lord and will continue to do so. For this reason, God has made a way for us to find forgiveness and acceptance through Jesus' atoning work on Calvary. When we confess our sins with a heart to turn from them, the blood of Jesus truly does wash away our sins and the accompanying guilt we feel. If we could begin to grasp this seemingly simple concept, I am totally convinced that we would see major changes within our lives and ministries.

"For I am not ashamed of the gospel, for *it is the power of God* for salvation to every one who believes..." (Romans 1:16). The gospel does not just contain the facts *about* the power of God but it *is* the power of God — "...for salvation..." The Bible is very clear that salvation is far more than being saved from hell — it is the entire redemption (from sin, sickness, the curse of the law, etc.) which Jesus purchased for us on the cross. The gospel *is* the *power* of God.

In practical terms, this means that by realizing and walking in God's grace each and every day, we will find far more power than by trying to live in our own strength. Beating on ourselves when we blow it yields no extra power to change. If we simply repent, however, and allow the mercies of the Lord to flood our being, we will find ourselves beginning to walk in His power, rather than in our own inconsistent strength.

"But God demonstrates His own love toward us, in that *while we were yet sinners*, Christ died for us" (Romans 5:8). Did the Lord call you into His kingdom? Did He forgive you when you were born again? Do you think that maybe, just maybe, He knew beforehand the failures you would commit after you became a Christian? Was He just toying with you then or is His forgiveness far-reaching enough to have effect even now? Obviously, even though He was fully aware of how you would fail, the Lord still called you into His kingdom. His grace is sufficient.

As you continue your walk with the Lord you will undoubtedly "blow it" again. It is not a question of living a perfectly sinless life. If we had the power to do that on our own then Jesus died for no reason. The real issue here is how we deal with our sin once we have committed it. Our natural tendency is to act as Adam did when he sinned and try to hide from God. We know we too have fallen short, and we feel that putting distance between ourselves and the Lord is the best way to handle it. Isn't that just like our sinful nature? We attempt to deal with the problem in a way that is totally opposite from God's way. He would have us turn to Him in repentance, even like the prodigal son, and find grace and forgiveness from our loving heavenly Father.

The third chapter of Ephesians helps drive home this point: "...that you, being rooted and grounded in love, may be able to comprehend with all the saints what is the breadth and length and height and depth, and to know the love of Christ which surpasses knowledge, *that you may be filled up to all the fullness of God*" (Ephesians 3:17-19). Being rooted and grounded in His love and knowing His love will cause us to be filled up to all the fullness of God. We are not filled up to all the fullness of God by working for Him more diligently. Even praying more or studying the Bible more will not fill us up to the fullness of God, although these will ultimately be by-products of knowing His love. We will be filled up to the fullness of God only when we comprehend and believe that God loves us as much as He does.

If we will learn that indeed His mercy can cover any failure, then it will be easier for us to continually believe He can use us. Seeing ourselves as holy and blameless in His sight will cause us to act differently. If we take the run-and-hide approach, we will find ourselves further from God each time we sin. But if, instead, we will run to the Lord, we will find a power that will make an ongoing difference within our lives and in our walk with the Lord. ❖

Chapter 7

Self-Discipline

What an awful chapter title: "Self-Discipline." I am certain that not many people want to hear about this topic, especially after reading the last chapter about God's grace. Discipline myself? It certainly does not sound like much fun to me.

It is true that self-discipline is not necessarily always fun, but it is essential. We must be willing to discipline ourselves in many areas — prayer, the study of God's Word, musical practice time, preparation for leading, etc. For me, this was and is one of the most difficult things about being a worship leader. It requires less effort to procrastinate, be lazy and be disorganized than it does to be organized, diligent and disciplined. It is easier for me to not practice my instrument and music than it is to apply myself diligently. It is much simpler for me not to pray than it is to truly intercede for those whom I lead in worship.

All of these areas require more than a half-hearted attitude in order to be truly effective. If I allow my flesh, my mood, or even the attitudes of others to dictate my discipline in these areas, I will not be the worship leader God has enabled me to be. I absolutely must discipline myself in order to be the worship leader God intends.

"Do you not know that those who run in a race all run, but only one receives the prize? Run in such a way that you may win" (I Corinthians 9:24). If we can put this in the current vernacular, Paul is telling us to "go for it!" This is not a time to be slothful; it is time to press forward in Jesus with all our might.

Paul's next statement is even stronger: "And everyone who competes in the games exercises self-control in all things. They then do it to receive a perishable wreath, but we an imperishable" (I Corinthians 9:25). We have far more at stake than earthly athletes. No, we will probably not lose our salvation if we do not discipline our lives, but we and others may miss our high callings in the Lord's kingdom if we take lightly the things He has entrusted to us.

Paul finishes out this line of thought with these words: "Therefore I run in such a way, as not without aim; I box in such a way, as not beating the air; but I buffet my body and make it my slave, lest possibly, after I have preached to others, I myself should be disqualified" (I Corinthians 9:26-27). A friend of mine points out that the word "buffet" here is not pronounced "buff-ay" as though we were feeding our sensual desires. It literally means to punch or fight. We need to bring our physical man into submission to what the Holy Spirit is asking of us.

It has been said that God can only use us to the extent that we are willing to discipline ourselves. In other words, He will not override our wills. Understanding the grace principle from the last chapter, as well as the sovereignty of God, makes this statement a little strong, but it still has value. God will not ordinarily bypass our wills in order to put His plans into action. Scripture does record times when the Lord has overridden or changed someone's will, but these times are more the exception than the rule. He requires that we be willing to put our will and effort into what He desires for us. Without them we will never fully achieve God's ultimate purpose for our lives.

I can hear the responses even as I write this, "But I have plenty of things to pray about in my own life, why do I need to take extra time to pray for those whom I lead?" "I would much rather sleep a little later on Sunday mornings than to get up so early just to prepare to lead." I could go on but I'm sure you get the point. Unless we are willing to buffet our bodies into submission, to discipline our lives, then we will never truly be effective in leading God's people in worship.

James 4:7 tells us much the same thing. In the first six verses of the chapter James rebukes the readers for giving in to worldly passions. Then he says, "Submit therefore to God. Resist the devil and he will flee from you." The words "submit" and "resist" are not passive. They demand action on our part. We cannot be complacent; we must discipline our lives. We must submit to the Lord's will and bring our own wills into submission.

We are wise if we pray regularly for those whom we lead as well as those with whom we minister. We are wise if we pray regularly for ourselves, asking that we might be sensitive to the Holy Spirit. We are wise if we work diligently at our music. These things and more are must-do's for those who aspire to be effective in leading God's people in worship.

Of course, this entire concept of self-discipline needs to be understood in light of the previous chapter. It is being rooted and grounded in God's grace and mercy that will give us the long-term ability to discipline our lives for maximum benefit to His kingdom. If we will follow His Word and willingly discipline ourselves we will become far more effective in the role to which He has called us. God will multiply our efforts at self-discipline even beyond our expectations. If we will take the first step, He will pour out His blessing. ❖

Chapter 8

Understanding God's Word

One of the most effective worship leaders I have ever met was the man who discipled me into leading worship. I did not really even fully understand worship, let alone leading worship, until I met him. He is an extremely gifted vocalist and instrumentalist. However, I am convinced that his effectiveness in leading worship stems more from his knowledge of God's Word than from his musical abilities.

I remember him frequently saying something like, "Let's sing Psalm 121, verses 1 through 4." The rest of us would stare blankly until he started the song and, of course, we all knew the song. We just did not know where it came from. Sometimes we would sing songs that I did not even realize were straight out of the Bible until he mentioned the reference. My point is not that he knew Scripture references for the songs we sang, but that he knew the Word. He had hidden God's Word in his heart. Therefore, he had a knowledge of God which many believers often lack.

Recently someone asked me a question which I had never really considered before. The question was this: "Is it more important for a full-time worship leader to have a music degree or a degree in Biblical studies?" Although I had never thought about this concept before I did not hesitate even a moment in answering. You see, I've seen and heard about so many worship leaders who have wreaked havoc within their congregations that, for me, there really is only one appropriate answer.

Very often worship leaders are in their position because they are gifted musically. They usually have a great deal of creativity and a thorough understanding of music and its use. What is too often lacking, though, is a thorough understanding of God, His ways and His dealings with people. Without this foundation in place, there are often major problems.

The following is a too-often repeated scenario: an immature but musically talented Christian is put in the position of worship leader at a church. He loves the Lord. Musically, he is amazing. In time, people begin to tell him what a good worship leader he is and how anointed he is. Unfortunately, because he does not have a solid Biblical foundation, he begins to believe them... too much so. He believes that he is so anointed that God must want him to be in charge. There follows either a major power struggle within the leadership of the church, or, possibly, a mass exodus to start a new church.

Now, obviously with this scenario a number of problems can be pointed out. First, the pastor was potentially wrong, because he did not more carefully consider the Biblical qualifications for this leadership position (I Timothy 3:1-7, and elsewhere). Somehow, for worship leaders these qualifications are often overlooked. Yet the worship leader is usually the second most prominent up-front minister in the church. Only the pastor is seen as "in-charge" more often than the worship leader within a church service. Frequently the worship leader, besides being the creative type, is outgoing and has a large measure of personal charm and charisma. In other words, he is usually a popular person. All of these ingredients mixed together can be dangerous. Do not ever underestimate such a worship leader's influence within the congregation.

Secondly, the pastor could have erred in another way. If it was essential, for whatever reasons, to put an immature Christian in this position, he should have at least been willing to disciple (teach, train, counsel, love, encourage, etc.) him on a regular basis. This would be the absolute minimum required under the circumstances.

Thirdly, the people in the congregation could have been guilty of giving too much praise to an individual. I am a strong believer in affirming people in their gifts, but sometimes a proper balance is hard to find. As long as the recipients of the praise remember Who ultimately gets the glory there is no problem. But sometimes we have a tendency to keep a little for ourselves which makes it easier for us to keep a little more the next time. Finally, we can end up so certain of our own abilities that we really have no need for God, or so we think. Too much praise can be destructive.

All of these potential errors on the part of others are valid. They need to be weighed and considered. Ultimately though, the responsibility falls back upon the worship leader to be a firm, solid Christian, who knows God through His Word. Putting all gifts, talents and callings aside for a moment, we must understand this very basic foundation. The Bible has within it all that we need to know about walking out the life which God has called us into. It teaches us of God's unsurpassable love and grace. It tells us to pray and seek God continually. It urges us to be diligent to repent and walk in holiness. Without a strong knowledge of and firm commitment to the truths which God has revealed in the Bible, no gift, no talent, no calling will ever bring about God's intended purposes. Period.

God's Word is the only reliable source of truth. It must be the final authority in all we believe and how we live. Absolutely nothing else will stand the test of time. I remember going to a movie as a little boy. We arrived early, so they let us go into the theater before the previous showing of the same movie had ended. When the show we came to see began, there was no doubt as to the outcome. I knew the end from the very start. God's Word is somewhat the same. It shows us His plan and His "end" before it unfolds. It enables us to keep ourselves and those we lead on track with the Lord and His plans.

Yes, musical talents are an important commodity for a worship leader. But even more essential to the worship leader is a thorough knowledge of God's Word. It is not absolutely necessary for a worship leader to have a degree in Biblical studies, but this would be a much better foundation than music training alone. Knowing God through His Word is an essential element in being an effective leader of worship. Knowing the Lord through His Word needs to be an extremely high priority for believers, but especially for worship leaders. ❖

Chapter 9

Accepting the Role of Being an Example

Years ago, when I first became part of the worship team at our church, I had a stunning realization. I remember well my reaction to people looking at me, the bass player on the worship team, as an example of a worshipping Christian. Quite simply, I hated it. I had absolutely no desire to be a role model. That was not the reason I had become a part of the music ministry at our church. I simply wanted to worship the

Lord with the gifts He had given me. But an example for others to follow... me?! No way!

I soon stumbled across this passage in Paul's letter to the church at Phillipi: "Brethren, join in following my example, and observe those who walk according to the pattern you have in us" (Philippians 3:17). "Well sure, Lord, but that is the Apostle Paul talking. Certainly You do not expect people to follow *my* example," I reasoned. But I realized that I really did not have much of a choice. Peoples' attitudes are such that if you minister in front of the church, even if you are just the bass player, you are considered a leader.

This is even more true for the worship leader. And, it even carries over into your "off" time. Regardless of where you are or what you are doing, people observe you to see what a worshipping Christian is really like. If you are playing with your kids at a park, people want to see how you act. If you are yelling at the manager of the local department store because of some ongoing problem, people will watch to see how a worshipping Christian behaves. Wherever you find yourself people will observe your actions. This is at least part of the reason why Scripture demands that leaders have their lives somewhat in order (I Timothy 3:1-13, etc.). Being an example even includes the entire concept of moral integrity. I have heard it said of worship leaders, or any leader for that matter, "Others may but you may not." As a leader your life needs to be exemplary.

This whole concept can be very unnerving unless you are prepared to have others view you as an example. (It can sometimes be unnerving even if you are prepared for it.) Few people like to accept the responsibility of being a model for others to follow. However, like it or not, being an example comes with the territory. If you are a worship leader, people will watch your example whether you want them to or not. I realized that it is easier just to accept this than to fight against it. Besides, if people can't watch us to see what a worshipper is really like, who can they watch?

David apparently understood this idea when he demonstrated his worship of God in front of all of Israel. "And David was dancing before the Lord with all his might..." as they brought the ark of the covenant back to Jerusalem (II Samuel 6:14-15).

King Solomon perceived the importance of being an example at the temple dedication. II Chronicles 6:13 tells us that Solomon built a large platform and knelt down on it "in the presence of all the assembly of Israel and spread out his hands toward heaven" and prayed. Unquestionably, the King wanted the people to see how he prayed. He was setting a pattern that the people could follow.

Paul again, in his second letter to the Thessalonians, said of himself and his companions that we "offer ourselves as a model for you, that you might follow our example" (II Thessalonians 3:9). Paul, probably more than anyone, understood how vital it is to have role models. Did he start out to be a role model? Probably not. Did he enjoy it? That answer is unclear. What is clear, however, is that Paul accepted the responsibility of being an example for others to follow.

People have a need to be taught, not only by your words but just as much by your actions. The "don't do as I do, do as I say" mentality must be removed from our way of thinking. We as worship leaders cannot just talk about worship being a way of life. We must live it. And we must live it to the extent that others can look at us and see what worshippers are really like. Refusing to accept this responsibility is not an option. Like it or not, people will learn from *your* example. ❖

Chapter 10

Cultivating the Gifts God Has Put Within You

God has given each one of us certain gifts to use for His glory. "But to *each one* is given the manifestation of the Spirit for the common good. For to one is given the word of wisdom..., to another the word of knowledge..., to another faith..., to another gifts of healing..., to another the effecting of miracles, and to another prophecy, and to another the distinguishing of spirits, and to another various kinds of tongues, and to another the interpretation of tongues. But one and the same Spirit works all these things, distributing to each one individually just as He wills" (I Corinthians 12:7-11).

There is no question that we have each been given at least one gift. The friction comes when we consider nurturing the gift(s). We would much rather simply wait for the Lord to act in a sovereign manner within our lives to make the gift come forth in its fullest potential. We really do not want to work at the gifts He has given us. We just want them to happen. Unfortunately, that's not the way the Lord designed it.

In writing to Timothy, his son in the faith, Paul exhorts, "...kindle afresh the gift of God which is in you through the laying on of my hands" (II Timothy 1:6). Another translation says to "stir up" the gift. "Kindle afresh." "Stir up." These are phrases demanding action. They require a response. But was not the gift already within Timothy? Was it not a gift from the Lord? Then why did Paul tell him to do something? Because that is how God has chosen to develop people's gifts.

"Even so ye, forasmuch as ye are zealous of spiritual gifts, *seek that ye may excel* to the edifying of the church" (I Corinthians 14:12). How can we seek to excel at the gifts of God unless we somehow have a part in developing them?

The Lord gives us gifts and then expects us to learn to use them to their fullest potential. Certainly He will lead us and guide us, but we have to work with the gifts to learn to "excel" at them. It is very rare, even in Scripture, for the Lord to sovereignly give a "full-blown" gift to someone.

In cultivating the gifts God has placed within you, do not neglect prayer. Faithful prayers have the ability to do far more than all of the other work we can do. And yet prayer alone is not all that the Lord requires. We must work diligently at the gifts which He has given so that when this life is over we may hear, "Well done thou good and faithful servant" (Matthew 25:21, 23).

In practical terms, we need to use and work at the gifts He has bestowed on us as leaders of worship. Do you have musical gifts? Have you continued to cultivate them and learn more? Do you practice your instrument on a regular basis? Depending on your level of proficiency, you should perhaps consider further music courses at a local junior college or from a private instructor or even by correspondence. Perhaps music theory would be in order or further lessons on your instrument(s). If you are experienced enough and have developed your gift to a high degree of expertise, maybe you should consider giving lessons. Regardless of the subject I almost always learn something when I have the opportunity to teach others.

Are you a would-be songwriter? Have you considered taking a music composition course? Perhaps a class on poetry or grammar would be in order. Maybe researching other song writers would be helpful. Even corresponding with some of today's writers of popular worship songs might be a worthwhile endeavor.

Has God given you the ability to be able to communicate effectively with others? Endeavoring to enhance this gift with a seminar on public speaking would be a good idea.

All of these things and more are there for the doing. Regardless of what your gifts are there is still room for improvement. God has already given us the gifts. How far we go with them is now up to us. ❖

Chapter 11

Keeping
Priorities Straight

I have found that one of the most difficult things for people to do in any area of life is to determine priorities. We all seem to have trouble at times deciding what is the greatest need of the moment. In my ten years in the sales field, this was my most common downfall. I often found it easier to do the more enjoyable aspects of my job than to do what was necessary at the moment. Please understand that I really liked my job. However, some parts were more fun than others. This is true in every area of life and we must decide that what is the most fun should not and will not ultimately determine how we appropriate our time.

God has clearly shown me that I have three main priorities:

1. Knowing Him and cultivating that relationship
2. Loving, spending time with and caring for my family
3. Laboring in the ministry which He sets before me

In order to determine what I should do at any given time, I mentally review this list to be certain that I am not being sidetracked. We have already discussed the first priority, maintaining a strong relationship with God, in chapter one. Priority number two is the one I personally seem to struggle with the most. I believe I struggle because I am a very "results-oriented" person. For example, I can usually see immediate results from teaching a worship seminar to fifty people. It is more difficult for me to see immediate results from praying with or playing with my son or taking my wife out to dinner. And yet these are as important, and often more important, in fulfilling God's plan for my life than doing more of "the ministry."

The long-term effect of spending time with my family will far outweigh a few hours of teaching worship leaders. My sons have the potential of having a far greater impact on the kingdom of God than I do. However, if I do not instill in them proper values and priorities now they will never reach their full potential in the Lord. No one else is going to take the responsibility for training my family — that is my job. If I prioritize correctly and spend the time with them, the long-term results will be well worth the effort.

Beyond my family, it is important that I model these priorities for the people on my music team. If they see that "ministry" is my main priority then they may end up emulating that. They need to *see* me having family as a top concern. If my wife and children stop by when we are rehearsing, I encourage my son to come in and give me a hug. Yes, it may disrupt our practice for a minute but he is a priority.

I also verbally encourage the worship team to see family as a priority. We have a rotating schedule for our music ministry team. Each person is scheduled to minister an average of three out of four Sundays. Being "on" when they are scheduled to be "off" is not an option. It is important that they spend time worshipping with their families. It is vital that they and their families see worship as not just an up-front ministry. It is healthy for the team members to spend time being normal congregational worshippers.

God is first. My family is second. My third priority is the ministry which God sets before me. Please note that this is not just any ministry, but that which the Lord is asking of me. It is not always easy to discern exactly which ministry opportunities are from the Lord, but it is important to attempt to understand. There have been times in the past when I jumped head first into any ministry opportunity that came along. I did not seek the Lord as to whether or not it was for me; I just did it. Then I realized that not every opportunity was from God. I needed to discern what *He* was asking me to do.

One simple way of beginning to discern whether or not something is from the Lord is to see if it preempts the first two priorities. Of course there may be times when a ministry trip may be inconvenient for my family and still be of God, but in the long term, my family must be a higher priority than the ministry.

Therefore, work to determine, understand, and implement Biblical priorities in your own life and ministry. With these in place, you will find yourself directed more by God and His will for you, rather than by the pleas of countless people and legitimate needs for your time. Jesus said in John

8:29: "...I always do the things that are pleasing to Him (the Father)." And He did not meet every felt need on earth. Realize that it is all right to say "No" to people's requests once in a while. Seek the Lord for His priorities in your life and then follow them. ❖

Chapter 12

Using and/or Cultivating Administrative Abilities

Without question, the thing most consistently lacking in the music ministries of churches I have visited is good administration. This is not to say that none of the music ministers have any administrative abilities. Overall, however, organization and administration have taken a back seat to nearly every other priority. My overall perception has been that this has at least one major contributing factor (and probably several minor ones, each one different in each different setting). The major reason for this administrative lack seems to be that the worship leader/minister of music/head of the music department is not primarily an administrator. Musical leaders usually are enlisted for their artsy, musical, creative abilities, not for their organizational prowess.

Today, it seems contradictory to be both creative and organized at the same time. This phenomenon seems, at least in part, to be due to the left-brain, right-brain functions. The right side of the brain generally governs the creative and artistic abilities, while the left side primarily controls organizational abilities. Unfortunately, many people in our society use this left/right-brain philosophy to justify a less than desirable performance in an area where they are undisciplined. It is understandable to us that a highly talented musician would be extremely disorganized. However, does being understandable make such behavior patterns excusable?

My pastor is an extremely gifted and creative musician. One day many years ago, God impressed upon him that it was time for him to get organized. He argued with the Lord that, since he was the artistic type, organization was pretty much out of the question. God asked him if he thought he was more creative than the Creator. The answer was obviously, "No." Then the Lord asked if he thought that He, God, was organized. My pastor has since worked earnestly on being more organized.

These two characteristics need not be mutually exclusive. It *is* possible to be a creative artist and to have administrative and organizational abilities. Certainly most people find one of these extremes easier to lean toward than the other, but either ability can be learned to a high degree of proficiency.

If you are a creative person and find organization and

administration repulsive, I believe that God has a word for you: "Change your attitude!" It is possible to develop organizational skills even if they do not come naturally. Practically speaking, you could take a class on administration at a local junior college. You could go to a "Getting Organized" seminar. Talk to friends who are more given to this kind of thinking and see if they have any advice for your specific situation. Seek the counsel of business people in your congregation about methods of organization which they have found to be helpful. Whatever methods you decide to use, you *need* to begin to develop organizational abilities. If you do not, your artistic flair may continue to blossom but you will never be organized enough for it to have the full impact God desires for it.

Another practical step you can take in getting organized is to have others help you in your administrative endeavors. In other words, delegate. Ask someone else to take on some of the more tedious organizational tasks such as filing music, keeping up with copyrights, etc. There may be administrative people who would like to help in organizing special services and in coordinating the various music department personnel. All of these are helpful, but they still do not negate the necessity of *your* achieving a level of organization. Without developing your administrative abilities you will never fully become the worship *leader* God wants you to be. ❖

Chapter 13

Caring For the Congregation

While I was in seminary, one of my professors drilled a statement into us which has become an ongoing foundation for much of what I do in ministry. The statement is this: "Don't just do your ministry, minister to people." It is easy for us to miss this seemingly simple idea in much of what we refer to as "ministry." We are often far more ready to accept the responsibilities of the work of ministry than we are to accept the responsibility of caring for people. The work and the doing of the work is important, but Jesus died for *people.*

For us as worship leaders, this ministry to people sometimes seems difficult to grasp. After all, our first priority is to worship the Lord. This is true, but if we see only worshipping the Lord as valuable, we have missed half of our job title: Worship *Leader.* We have a responsibility to *lead* people in worship.

The title of this chapter, "Caring for the Congregation," refers to seeing the needs of those to whom we are ministering as more important than our own needs. "Do nothing from selfishness or empty conceit, but with humility of mind *let each one of you regard one another as more important than himself"* (Philippians 2:3). For example, on a given Sunday you may feel like celebrating with great exuberance before the Lord. However it is obvious that what the congregation needs is to bask in the presence of the Lord in intimate worship. Which way do you go?

Placing the needs of others above your own is not always comfortable. There have been instances during a time of worship when I was uncertain as to which direction to go. At that point I decided I had two choices. I could either stand there and act as if I had it all together, or I could leave the platform and consult with the pastor and other leaders regarding the direction of the service. If I chose to pretend I was "in control," the people would probably miss something God wanted them to experience. If I chose to leave the platform for consultation, there was the potential for people to view me as weak and not "together." Really, there was no choice. The people were too important for me to care about my feelings or reputation. I desired God's very best for them.

"Caring for the congregation." It means lovingly encouraging them to follow along as you start up the mountain to God's presence. Do not beat them. Gently coax them to come on along. They get enough abuse every day from the world. From you they need encouragement.

Our natural tendency, if the people seem to be slow in following our leadership is something like this, "Hey! Are you guys awake out there?!" This may be effective once or twice, but in the long term we need to take a different approach. What people need is loving, caring encouragement. This will cause them to follow your leadership over the long haul better than anything else. Try encouraging them instead of provoking them.

"Caring for the congregation." It means listening to and responding to comments and suggestions from people. For example, if over a period of one month 20 people tell you that they think, "We're doing too many fast songs," maybe, just maybe, you should consider the possibility that you are doing too many fast songs. Now obviously you cannot tailor the worship experience to fit the preferences of one person or even a small group of people, but it is important to hear feedback from those to whom you are ministering.

It should be noted that this type of feedback will usually be negative. I have found from personal experience that people tend to act and react in a similar manner regardless of the setting. The unhappy minority speak out while the contented majority sit silently. The average worship leader probably receives as many as 20 "suggestions" for change for every one positive comment. Does that mean he is doing a poor job? Usually not. People tend to speak out only when they are dissatisfied. In order to guard your own heart, you must understand that negative feedback is common.

The natural tendency for a criticized leader is to tell his/her critics that they are wrong and that he/she is right. This, however, is dangerous. If your job is to lead the congregation in worship, then you need to hear their reactions to what you are doing. Without knowing their response you will never know for certain whether you are fulfilling your responsibility of leading or if it is just you that is worshipping.

In all of these things remember that one of your primary responsibilities is to the members of your congregation. Sometimes they do not respond as you would like. Sometimes they say things you would rather not hear. Yet, they are the people the Lord has called you to lead in worship. Love them and encourage them in all you do. ❖

Chapter 14

Choosing Members for Your Worship Team

At some point you will probably reach the point of realizing that you could use some instrumental and/or vocal help in leading worship. When this happens and you decide to form a worship team (praise team, music ministry team, etc.) then you will need some ideas on choosing the right people. Here are a few thoughts.

First of all, pray!!!!! I am still uncertain as to whether I have put enough exclamation marks after that word. When choosing your team, prayer must be the number one priority. If you miss this principle the rest of these ideas will be worthless. That settled, the question is, "So what do I pray about?"

First, pray that the Lord will either raise up the right people within your congregation or send the right people to your congregation. Be specific in this prayer. What do you need? A drummer? A bass player? A pianist? Will just any pianist do or should they have a certain level of skill? What about their heart attitude? What about their commitment to the Lord and to your church? If these things are important, then make them prayer priorities. The Lord honors specific prayers.

Second, pray for wisdom and sensitivity to the Holy Spirit. You, as the worship leader, will make the final decision about who is a part of the team. Even more than having good human ideas you need to tap into the mind of Christ (I Corinthians 2:16).

Qualities to Look For In Prospective Music Team Members

Maturity is the first thing I look for in individuals whom I am considering for our worship team. I am not as interested in physical maturity as I am their spiritual maturity. Do they really *know* God? Have they been walking with Him for a long time? If I do not know the individual personally, I talk to those whom I trust and are mutual acquaintances. I want as much information going into the relationship as possible. Six months after they are a part of the team is not the best time to find out that they have some major areas of immaturity.

The next quality I look for is commitment, both to the Lord and to our congregation. Is this person not only mature but a solid believer? And, are they strongly committed to the work where they will be ministering? There are enough jump-from-church-to-church Christians with the body of Christ in general, we certainly do not need them on our worship team.

Finally, I look at their musical abilities. Please notice that this is the third quality that I look for and not the first. The other two are far more important. However, musical abilities are important. Musicians need to be skilled enough to follow a service which is "led by the Holy Spirit." Poor musical abilities can distract and detract from the people's worship.

Clear and Constant Communication

This is probably the biggest point of downfall in the entire area. If you communicate clearly you can avoid lots of problems. If you do not communicate clearly, you are simply setting yourself and your team up for trouble later on.

I believe in written guidelines for worship teams. I have compiled a sheet with a complete list of what is expected of members of our worship team (i.e., time commitment, spiritual maturity, family acceptance, attitude, etc.). When someone talks to me about being a part of our team I simply hand them the sheet. I tell them if they are still interested after reading the guidelines we will sit down and talk. Over half of the people who have expressed interest have never broached the subject again. They read the guidelines, understood the commitment, and realized it was not for them. What would have happened if we had no written guidelines and they had joined the team? Then it would have been too late for them to realize the commitment was too great.

Communication is vital all the way through the process of choosing team members (as well as afterwards). If you decide an applicant is to be a part of the team, they need to know exactly what that means, what their role will be, etc. If they are not to be a part of the team let them know that too. Communicate, you will be glad you did.

In all of these things keep the first thing we discussed in this chapter in mind. Pray!!!! This will alleviate most problems before they start and help you locate the people the Lord wants to be a part of your worship team. ❖

Chapter 15

Caring for the Members of Your Worship Team

From my earliest recollections of being a part of our church's worship team (over twelve years ago) I remember very vividly that we were friends. We spent time together. We enjoyed one another's company. We even liked each other. To this day, we still are friends.

It was not until I began to travel regularly and minister at other churches that I realized what a different concept this is. In my travels I have seen everything from situations similar to ours, to people who tolerate each other, to others who actually despise one another. I have talked to some worship leaders who feel as though no one on their team really cares about them as a person. They feel as though they cannot communicate their overall goal for worship to the other members of the team. There is strife in the practice sessions, and there is even friction on Sunday mornings. Some have even told me they want to quit.

What a tragedy that too often they have not realized the importance of cultivating good, solid, Biblical relationships. This can effectively alleviate most worship team problems. No, problems will not necessarily completely disappear, but they can be minimized by having proper relationships. It is an amazing fact that cultivating good, solid relationships will enhance everything in your music ministry program.

For example, if I feel that our lead guitarist needs to do a heart check about his motivation for the way he is playing lately, it will be received much better if that person is my friend. If, on the other hand, the only time I ever talk to him is when I feel I need to correct something, he will be far less open to my correction.

If the only way you ever interact with the members of your worship team is on a "professional" level, then you are missing a big part of what the Lord wants to do within your group. Loving, caring, friendly relationships should permeate everything you do as a team. Relationships like this can even help you do better musically. Friends desire to see one another do their very best. They help each other to reach their highest potential in God, even musically.

It is obvious from both Scripture and experience that wrong attitudes toward one another within the congregation can be a hindrance to worship. God is building His people into a temple to offer up spiritual sacrifices, or worship (I Peter 2:5). If the building is not built with right relationships then the spiritual sacrifices offered in that temple will be lacking. This effect is magnified if the poor relationships are among the members of the worship ministry team, a microcosm of the congregation as a whole. The main responsibility of the team is the area of worship. If there is constant discord within the team, then the praise and worship will suffer greatly.

So how do you cultivate strong, solid relationships on the worship team? First, the team members must decide that they desire and will earnestly pursue such relationships. This commitment may not be easy, and it may not always be exciting. The final result, however, is well worth the price.

Some practical ideas are actually very simple. Invite the team members (not necessarily everyone at once) over for dinner. In so doing you are with them on a social basis, not just a professional one. This will allow you to get to know one another as people, not only as musicians. We have an annual cook-out for the members of our worship team *and their families*. We get together and eat, play volleyball, eat, talk, eat, play party ping pong, and eat. It is strictly social and a lot of fun. And it does wonders for our overall relationships.

We also take time to enjoy one another's company at our rehearsals. This was hard for me to handle at first since I am a time-conscious, administrative type. But as I have realized how vital our relationships with one another are, I have seen the necessity of having fun together. So our practices are not strict regimented times. We take time to enjoy one another.

The following are some other practical ideas. First, keep up on the personal lives of your team members. Find out how they are doing at home and work. Send them birthday cards (preferably on their birthdays). Let them know you care about them as people. Because of the fine home fellowship group system which we have at our church I do not feel a need to offer daily pastoral guidance. However, if one of the members of our music team is hurting, I am quick to find out how I can help.

Also, let the team members know how *you* are doing. People will be quicker to open up to you when you lead the way by being open and honest with them first. Transparency needs to start with someone. It might as well be you. After all, you are the worship leader.

Understand that you may not see eye-to-eye with all team members on every issue. Absolute agreement is not necessary. What *is* necessary is that you remember an even more vital principle than the one on which you disagree; and that is Jesus' command to love one another. It is a much higher motivation to love and care for each other, even when you do not feel like it, than to simply tolerate one another.

Cultivate friendship within your worship team. You will be amazed at what a positive overall effect it can have. ❖

Chapter 16

Getting the Most Out of Your Rehearsals

Many churches have asked about practical ideas for their worship team rehearsals/preparation times. Often practice times can become mundane and, honestly, boring for the participants. I cannot necessarily offer the final word on how to handle these sessions, but I will try to offer a few practical tips.

First, one of the major questions is, "How often should

we get together as a team?" There are no right and wrong answers to this question since there are so many variables involved. Your decision must be determined by your situation. Practically speaking, a once-a-week practice works best in most cases. But working together musically is difficult in a given service if you are not *very* familiar with one another's abilities and musical styles. The ability to "flow" together as a team is made possible in large part by working together often. Without this regular interaction it will be difficult, at best, to be "tight" musically.

The length of the practice session should also be determined by your particular circumstances. A team which consists of two musicians will probably not require as much time as a thirty piece orchestra. Be careful, however, to keep in mind that as your team grows your practices may need to be longer. This is important to remember so that you do not lock yourself into a certain practice length now, and, if and when you change it, end up with disgruntled musicians. Let them know that there may come a time when your preparation times may have to change.

Another common question is, "What should we do at our rehearsals?" On the surface, the answer would seem obvious. However, by looking a little further one can reveal some unconsidered ideas. I have listed several below, but keep in mind that all of these do not necessarily need to be a part of every practice. They can be intermixed and used at appropriate times to accomplish the necessary agenda.

1. Worship. This is often an overlooked part of the practice time. It is difficult to lead in worship on Sunday mornings as a team if we never worship together at any other time. Our job is not just to provide a musical background whereby others may worship — we are to be the leaders in worship. If our times of preparation consist only of "doing music" and not actually worshipping God ourselves, we are sending the wrong message to our musicians. We are telling

them that the music aspect is more important than what is coming from the heart. Spending time in worship together as a team is vital.

2. Prayer. This too is frequently left out of many practice times. We should take time to pray for one another, for the congregation, for the pastor, etc. Pray and seek God's direction together for a particular service or series of services. All of these are important in building team unity.

A good thing to remember as the leader is striking a balance in your participation in the times of prayer. You should be an example for the others in prayer, without making it your time of prayer. Do not dominate the entire time by praying aloud and not allowing the others to pray also. Encourage them to "make their requests known" (Philippians 4:6).

3. New songs. Finally we get to what everyone thinks practices are all about. Please keep in mind, though, that this is number three on the list.

When attempting to learn new songs it is usually best to have music for all musicians. Some may be able to share, but asking twelve musicians to gather around one hand-scrawled 3x5 note card is a bit much.

Some teams prefer to have separate vocalist and instrumentalist sessions when learning new songs. This helps them learn vocal harmonies and various instrumental parts without interfering with one another. This, again, will depend upon your particular situation.

One important note on this: always try to learn a song thoroughly before using it corporately. This can save a great deal of embarrassment for everyone. On the other hand, it should be understood that working on a given song for months without using it for a corporate service can be very frustrating for the worship team members.

4. Old songs. This is especially important if you add new people to your worship team. Most people simply assume

that the new people know all of the old songs. Unfortunately, this is rarely the case. It is good to have a "working list" of songs and occasionally be certain that everyone on the team is familiar with all of these songs.

It is also worthwhile to sometimes take an old song and do a new musical arrangement for it. This can go a long way toward bringing new life to something old.

5. Evaluate previous service(s). This can be very helpful as long as you do not become introspective. Looking at what you did musically as well as considering the overall response from the congregation can be beneficial for future reference. Reviewing previous services is not so you can repeat something that worked last time but to evaluate why things happened the way they did and what potentially could have been done differently. This is not a time to be super-critical. Simply look at what happened for the purpose of learning. A great deal can be learned from sincere evaluation.

6. Special music. These songs usually involve a bit more work than the praise and worship songs partially because the special music is often more intricate but also because the congregation will not be singing. They only listen. Most churches will spend more time "polishing" their special music than they do with their praise and worship music.

One of my major considerations in all of these things is variety. Most people easily fall into predictable patterns in any area of life. This is true even in worship rehearsals. It is important to keep the interest and the enthusiasm of your musicians at a high level on an ongoing basis. This can be at least partially accomplished by adding variety and thereby avoiding falling into a rut in your worship rehearsals.

The ideas I suggested are not necessarily all-inclusive. There are probably numerous other practical suggestions you know about or are presently using. Combine your ideas with these and even add in some ideas from other people to find the proper balance for *your* rehearsals. ❖

Chapter 17

Understanding the Purposes for Music

It is amazing to me how many times the Bible refers to music. With over 800 references throughout Scripture it is obvious that music is something dear to the heart of God. If this is true, we should be as thoroughly familiar with its usage as possible. However, I have found that too often the people in charge of music in many churches seem ignorant of the great variety of uses the Word of God gives for music.

Let's take a look at a few of these.

The first, especially from our vantage point as worship leaders, should be obvious — to praise and worship the Lord. I believe that this is the highest purpose for music. Again and again, especially throughout the book of Psalms, we are entreated to "Praise the Lord!" and to "Sing unto the Lord!" Music is a wonderful way to give expression of our adoration to our Creator, Redeemer, Deliverer, Shelter, Helper in time of need. He is worthy of our praise.

Another use of music is to teach God's Word. "Let the Word of Christ richly dwell within you, with all wisdom teaching and admonishing one another with psalms and hymns and spiritual songs, singing with thankfulness in your hearts to God" (Colossians 3:16). We in the body of Christ today often know more Scripture because of the choruses we sing than we do through rote memorization. There is something about putting music with the words that makes them much easier for us to remember.

We can also help release God's power through music. In Acts 16 when Paul and Silas were in jail, they "...were praying and *singing hymns of praise to God*... and suddenly there came a great earthquake..." (Acts 16:25-26). Coincidence? I don't think so. In II Chronicles 20 three armies "came to make war against Jehoshaphat" (II Chronicles 20:1). After prayer and seeking the Lord, Jehoshaphat sent the singers out ahead of the army. "And when they began *singing and praising*, the Lord set ambushes against the [enemy] who had come against Judah; so they were routed" (II Chronicles 20:22). I do not fully understand how this works, but I have seen it happen too many times to believe it is just coincidence. It is not uncommon to experience physical and emotional healings, deliverances, salvations, etc. as we worship the Lord. God's power is somehow released through our music.

Music is also given to tell of God's great works and, consequently, to stir up our faith. "... tell of His works with joyful singing" (Psalm 107:22). Musically etching the works of God into our memories causes them to become more real to us. Even the children of Israel seemed to comprehend this when the Lord brought them out of Egypt. "Then Moses and the sons of Israel sang this song to the Lord, and said, 'I will sing to the Lord, for He is highly exalted; the horse and its rider He has hurled into the sea...'" (Exodus 15:1). We can do this with the works the Lord does among us today. What would happen if we wrote songs that told of the miracle healing He performed in our church service two weeks ago? Would it help us to remember and give Him praise? "I will give thanks to the Lord with all my heart; I will tell of all Thy wonders" (Psalm 9:1).

Music also helps bring a unity within our services. As we gather together we each come from varied backgrounds and experiences. This makes it nearly imperative for us to have a vehicle whereby we can all more easily focus on Jesus. There is something about music that aids us in this focusing of our hearts and thoughts. It draws us together into a corporate unity more quickly than anything else can.

There are numerous other uses of music which we could discuss, but for the sake of brevity I will list only one other. Music prepares the hearts of the people to receive God's Word through the sermon. I have heard this use of music likened to a farm field. As we lead the people in praise and worship to the Lord we are, in effect, plowing up the soil of their hearts. Then the sower (the preacher) plants the seed of the Word. Nothing will work better than music for this preparation of the hearts. Be careful, however, not to make this your main focus during worship. Our eyes are to be on Jesus, not the upcoming message.

The main point here is to be open to the various ways that music can be used. Do not just have a single mindset and miss the other ways in which the Lord may use music. He knows no bounds. His creativity is limitless. ❖

Chapter 18

Understanding Music as a Tool

My father was an extremely talented person. He had the ability to do auto repair work, woodworking, electrical work, plumbing, etc. and all with a very high degree of professionalism. Having done all of these kinds of things for years, he had accumulated quite a collection of tools. He had more tool *boxes* full than I have tools. (Unfortunately, I did not inherit much of his ability to work with his hands. I did, however, learn a lot from him.) It always amazed me that regardless of the task, he had just the right tool to do the job. He very seldom used a tool to accomplish something for which it was not intended. He used the *right* tool for the job.

We as worship leaders need to understand this concept in our music. Some time ago I had the opportunity to attend a production featuring a major symphony orchestra. Throughout the evening nearly the entire gamut of human emotion was portrayed using only musical instruments. There was peace, there was joy, there was sorrow, there was tension. Each was depicted by the use of appropriate instrumentation. It was interesting to note that this would have been impossible to do had all of the instruments played continuously throughout the entire concert. Instead, the various instruments helped to create the proper setting and feel for what the music attempted to convey.

We in the church need to learn some of these concepts. We need to begin to be more sensitive with our use of music. Do not just "plow through" during your praise and worship time. Instead, strive to be sensitive to how you might enhance the moving of the Holy Spirit through the use of your music. A good friend of mine drives home the point, "Most church praise and worship music is put through a 'blander.' It all comes out sounding the same!" If it all sounds at least somewhat similar, we are not adequately expressing the various moods of the Spirit of God. There must be variety in what we do.

To that end, we need to learn to use each of the instruments we have available as tools. Just as my father used certain tools at certain times, it is necessary for us to choose carefully which instruments will most effectively portray what we are trying to say with our worship. If we are in a slow, intimate time of communing with the Lord, a blaring electric guitar solo or loud cymbal crashes would probably be out of order. On the other hand, during a boisterous time of jubilant celebration these things might be very appropriate. Obviously these are extreme cases, but we need to learn even subtle nuances of musical enhancement of our worship. Use *all* of the instruments you have available to their fullest potential, but do not overuse them.

In doing this we as worship leaders again need to be willing to be examples. I usually lead worship with my guitar. However, there are times, more and more frequently, that I do not even play. This is not because I do not know the music, but because the guitar would not work as well as another instrument to portray the "mood" of the song. Even vocally there are times when I stop singing or at least back off from my microphone. Sometimes it is because the song needs the soft intimacy of one of our female vocalists. Other times it may be because I feel that the congregation needs to hear one another worshipping the Lord instead of the up-front singers.

Before I ask others to sit out from playing or singing, I must first be willing to sit out myself. It is easier for me to tell our drummer to sit out the first two times through an intimate chorus if he has seen me sitting out on other songs.

The bottom line is this: we need to learn to be sensitive and creative with our music in order to enhance what God wants to do. If we simply blanderize our music we will miss at least part of the purpose of the Lord for us and our ministries. ❖

Chapter 19

Understanding the Power of Music

I mentioned earlier that I spent 10 years in sales before entering full-time ministry. During the last half of that time I sold commercial and industrial lighting products. In endeavoring to do the best job that I could, I did a great deal of research on lighting. The effects of light on people are truly amazing. For example, one of the main reasons that there are more suicides in the winter is because of the lack of sunlight.

Various types and degrees of lighting can also affect your buying habits. Even in the work place different types of lighting can make people work differently. If mere lighting has such a powerful effect on people, how much more will music. While lighting can make a strong impact, nothing in the "natural" realm can compare with the effect of music.

Music in and of itself is a powerful force. Even before adding the anointing of the Holy Spirit there seems to be some type of force in music itself. Music will affect your mood. It will alter your buying habits. It can help relieve pain. It can reduce or increase stress. It can make you work more efficiently. It can even affect your eating habits. Secular studies alone have proven all these things about music.

The Bible confirms the power of music. David played his harp for the tormented King Saul and the evil spirit from God departed (I Samuel 16:23). It says nothing about David singing, only that he played his harp. Music can even stir up the gift of prophecy. In II Kings 3:15 Elisha requested that a minstrel play before he would prophesy. I Samuel 10:5, 6, 10 refers to a group of prophets with "harp, tambourine, flute and a lyre before them." And when Saul met them he began to prophesy too. Are all of these events just coincidence? No, God has apparently put an inherent quality in music that gives it some sort of sway over the unseen realm. This is true for both good and evil purposes.

So what does all of this have to do with us as worship leaders? I believe that it is absolutely essential for us in this hour to begin to understand the power of music and to learn how to use it effectively. Music during an altar service is not just "mood music." It can dramatically affect people's lives.

We need to begin to find through personal experience and the experiences of others how to use music to its fullest potential. I am not talking only about instrumental sensitivity, although this will play into it. I am referring to finding out how music relates to what the Lord is doing and then using it to accomplish His purposes. I will be the first to admit that I have more questions in this area than answers. I do not fully understand how to always accomplish this in my own church, let alone in yours. However, I have no question that we have only begun to scratch the surface of the full potential of music. We may find some of the answers in music training, but we will undoubtedly find more answers on our faces before the One Who created music. He understands this vehicle we call music far better than all of our human teachers combined. Allow His creativity and sensitivity to fill you so that you can fulfill His purposes in the earth.

Let us continue to seek Him for the ways He would have us use the might which He has given us in music. ❖

Chapter 20

Compiling a Solid Song Repertoire

O pinions on songs and styles of music are usually not too hard to come by. Everyone has a thought on what is "good" music and what is "bad" music. I frequently hear comments like, "We do too many fast songs" or "we do too many slow songs." Some tell me that we do not sing enough hymns while others say that we sing too many hymns. There are those who feel that we do too many new songs and, of course, others feel that we fail to learn enough new songs. Everyone, and I do mean everyone, has an opinion.

The main key I have found to solve this problem is striking a balance and incorporating a variety of music and types of songs into the repertoire. If I am hearing both sides of the same issue expressed (i.e., "too many fast" and "too many slow") I figure I am probably just about where I should be musically.

Here are some practical ideas you can use in compiling a solid song repertoire.

The first thing I recommend is to examine the lyrics of old songs and potential new songs. It is best to examine the lyrics separately from the music because we musicians can often be swayed toward a song that is lyrically poor if the music is great. This is not a good idea. When checking the words, the following are a few things to look for:

• Do the words line up with Scripture? (Be careful to check the context.)

• Are they within the experience and understanding of the congregation? (Many 300 year old songs are not.)

• Do they rhythmically fit the music? (This is a real problem as more and more people who have very little training endeavor to write songs.)

Additionally, you should examine the music.

• Is the music good quality? (Not trite, boring, etc.)

• Is the music within the experience and understanding of the congregation? (Again, the music of many 300 year old songs is not, but neither is the music of many ultra modern songs.)

• Does it enhance the words? (The words "weeping and mourning and gnashing of teeth" sung to the tune of "The Joy of the Lord is My Strength" would probably not work well.)

You should also check for overall variety within your song repertoire.

• Do you use enough different keys in your music? (The congregation can easily become musically bored if you play everything in the key of C.)

• What about a variety of rhythms and tempos? (Fast, slow, 4/4, 2/4, 3/4, 6/8, etc.)

• Do you try different styles of music? (Y'all use any country music? Or hymns?)

• Do you introduce different types of songs? (The Bible talks about psalms and hymns and spiritual songs. Also there are prayers, praises, testimony songs, old songs, new songs, choruses, complex songs, etc.)

• Is there variety within individual songs? (Men sing, women sing, children sing, soloist sings, congregation sings, instrumental section, crescendo, decrescendo, modulate to a different key, etc., preferably not all in the same song!)

Constantly be on the lookout for new songs. The Bible repeatedly tells us to "sing a new song to the Lord." I am convinced that this is more for our benefit than for His: the Lord never tires of our saying "I love You," but we tire of saying it in exactly the same way with the same melody. We have a need to sing new songs. And with the many sources for new songs (see appendix at the back of this book), we have the advantage of being able to be very selective. Do not just use any song that happens along. Be careful to choose the right ones for the Lord's current dealings with your church.

Finally, be open to writing songs and sharing them. You, as the leader of worship in the congregation, understand the spiritual condition of your people. Knowing this, the Lord may well prompt you to write a song that is exactly what they need.

In all of these things, be careful to consider the opinions expressed by members of the congregation regarding the music you use. Remember not to take criticism personally, since it usually does not represent the opinion of the majority.

However, hear and acknowledge their opinion, for they are the ones you lead before the Lord. ❖

Chapter 21

Loyalty to Those in Authority Over You

Recently my pastor, Nick Ittzes, and I had the opportunity to be speakers for elective sessions during a major worship conference. We each spoke a couple of times on totally unrelated topics. Unknowingly, we each used the other several times as an example in our teachings. We spoke of each other with respect and admiration.

Over the three days of the conference numerous people

mentioned to me that they had attended sessions by each of us. The comments they made were all similar; they were amazed at our relationship and our mutual admiration for one another. Those were their words. What they were expressing was a longing to have a similar relationship with their pastors. They realized that the relationships which they had with their pastors were far from perfect, and they longed to see improvement.

Pastors and worship leaders can have solid, fulfilling relationships, but it is not necessarily easy. I have heard it likened to a marriage relationship. The pastor, just as the husband, is the one with ultimate authority. That does not mean he lords it over the worship leader, but he is in charge. He has ultimate responsibility for that particular congregation of people. The worship leader, just as the wife, must learn to be submissive. This is not always easy for a creative, "artsy" type person. But then, God never told us relationships would be easy. Sometimes the really important things in life require some real work.

I believe the most important characteristic a worship leader must pursue in relation to his pastor is loyalty, not a simple one-time verbal assent of loyalty, but a daily walking out of that loyalty. Developing loyalty may not necessarily be simple. Like love and faithfulness in a marriage, loyalty is a decision. It does not just happen; you must work at it. In practical terms, you can put aside your own plans and agendas and adopt the pastor's instead. You can willingly accept the pastor's comments and constructive criticism without it adversely affecting your relationship. You can decide that anything short of obvious rebellion against the Lord is not worth causing strife in your relationship. You can decide that no matter what happens, you will remain loyal.

"Obey your leaders, and submit to them; for they keep watch over your souls, as those who will give an account. Let them do this with joy and not with grief, for this would be unprofitable for you" (Hebrews 13:17).

I am convinced more and more that this is an extremely foreign concept within our society and culture. We do not really understand the full ramifications of the word loyalty. We accept being loyal until something happens which tests that loyalty, at which point we doubt that it is really worth the effort. However, we absolutely must convince ourselves that just as in a Biblical marriage relationship, loyalty in our relationship with our pastor is well worth the effort.

If you can find it within yourself to maintain this attitude, you will find something else very interesting happening at the same time. When your pastor realizes that you are loyal to him, he will begin to give you more freedom in your area of responsibility. This may seem a bit odd, but it is true. When your pastor sees that you are intensely loyal to him, he has no reason to fear what you might say or do. He will begin to trust you like never before.

To understand this, try viewing the situation from the pastor's perspective for a moment. In most congregations the worship leader is the second most influential person during the corporate gatherings. As much as one-third to one-half of the service time is taken up by your leadership. Put that concept into the mind of the pastor along with a few horror stories about worship leaders who have wreaked havoc within their congregations, and you have a very volatile mixture. But, if you as a worship leader can demonstrate your loyalty in tangible ways, the pastor will soon come to realize that he has nothing to fear from you.

A word of caution is definitely in order. Demonstrating loyalty for the sake of getting more freedom will not work. It is almost always obvious whether the loyalty is true, heart-felt loyalty or the I'm-doing-this-to-get-something type. Loyalty is not the means to achieve something; it is simply a necessity which we must cultivate within our lives. More freedom in ministry, given by the pastor, is simply a by-product of genuine intense loyalty.

There is another, perhaps in some ways even more important, principle at work here — that of sowing and reaping. I have found this to be absolutely true within my own experience. Because I have sown loyalty I have reaped loyalty. In visiting churches across the nation I have repeatedly heard negative comments, even in a public setting, from musicians about their worship leader. Although I find this very distressing, it is also somewhat comforting for me to know, without any doubt, that my musicians would never do this. They are 100 percent committed to my leadership. They are loyal to me, at least in part because I have been loyal to those over me. You *will* reap what you sow.

If you have not already done so, decide today that you will be loyal to your pastor. The final results of God's blessing on the congregation will be well worth the effort. ❖

Chapter 22

Sticking With It Even in the Not-So-Fun Times

I am frequently asked whether or not I ever get discouraged about leading worship. My usual response is, "Not since last Sunday!" The truth is that leading worship, although it is *often* a lot of fun, is not *always* a lot of fun. Sometimes it is just plain hard work. Sometimes it is even very discouraging. I challenge anyone who has led worship for over one year to tell me truthfully that they have never had a time of discouragement or disillusionment in leading. It is simply a natural part of life.

There have been times when I have prayed and sought the Lord regarding a specific service. I knew I had the mind of God for the service and was fully prepared to lead the people in an awesome time of worship. I could picture all of us caught up in the wonder and majesty of Almighty God. We would probably be so lost in the Lord that we would go on worshipping for hours. There was one minor problem in the whole plan — no one told the people. Now, I like to put the best construction on things. Probably what happened was that it was the middle of winter, the sun had not shone in weeks, and everyone had just received notice from the I.R.S. that their taxes were being audited. Whatever the reasons, the people were almost completely unresponsive. It was as if they did not even understand what worship was all about. Discouraging? You bet.

There have been other times when members of the music team or the sound crew have not displayed the type of commitment which I would like to have seen. Often I have been disappointed in team members only to discover later that if I had been in their situation, I would have made a similar choice. Although my attitude changed when I realized their circumstances, at the time it was discouraging.

Still other times we as a music team have worked for weeks on what we believe to be a "hot" new song. Then, with great anticipation, we introduce the song to the congregation. Lo and behold, they seem to like it so much that they cannot wait until we finish singing it so we can move on to the next song. Me... discouraged? Ha!

I have even heard several worship leaders refer to the "Sunday afternoon let-down syndrome." This is a feeling of mild depression following shortly after the service. I am uncertain as to whether this is completely psychological, somewhat physiological, or even partly spiritual. It could be related to everything from feelings of inadequacy because of the mistakes to the withdrawal from the adrenaline "high" during the service. Regardless, many worship leaders (and even pastors) experience this phenomenon regularly, and they find it very discouraging.

In all of these things it is important to remember why we do what we do. If we strive for popularity, fun times, goose bumps or anything except to serve God, we need to reconsider our motivation.

I once heard a midwestern pastor say that if he had taken a step west every time he had considered quitting the ministry, he would be in the Pacific Ocean by now. If I did the same thing I would probably have walked at least half way around the earth by now. But each time I think about giving up I realize that I am not leading worship just to have fun. Oh sure, there are lots (and I do mean *lots*) of fun times, but they are not the thing that got me started, nor will they keep me going long term. I am absolutely convinced that the Lord has called me, and He will sustain me.

In any part of life there will be trials. This is a simple fact of life. "Many are the afflictions of the righteous; but the Lord delivers him out of them all" (Psalm 34:19). God is most interested in how we handle the trials. I cannot base my walk with the Lord or even my service to Him on how things seem to be going in my life. There is only one standard I can safely measure against — the Word of God. If I ever begin to rely on good times, people's reactions or anything but the strength of the Lord to carry me through, I have ultimately missed God's best for me.

When I get discouraged or feel like quitting I remember some of His promises. He who has called me is faithful and He will see me through (I Thessalonians 5:24). "Weeping may endure for a night, but joy cometh in the morning" (Psalm 30:5). God is with me and will not forsake me in my time of need (Hebrews 13:5). "...He who began a good work in you will perfect it..." (Philippians 1:6). Amen. ❖

Chapter 23

Ministering Beyond Your Comfort Zone

"You don't have to like it, you just have to do it." How clearly those words from my childhood still ring within me. I disliked hearing them at the time because they often meant that I had to do something which left me, at the very least, uncomfortable. I did not like to be uncomfortable.

Incredibly, however, I find myself now using those same words occasionally with my oldest son. I also use them on myself, even in the arena of being a worship leader. There are times when I must go beyond what is comfortable for me. Sometimes this is ultimately for my benefit, and sometimes it is to help others achieve all that God has for them.

Several years ago I began to realize that God had called me not only to lead His people in worship, but also to disciple others into a worship leading role. In doing this I have encountered those who simply cannot do things the same way that I do. For example, I usually lead worship using my guitar. A couple of the people I have worked with over the years, although they are fine vocalists, play no musical instruments. "So how, Lord," I have asked, "am I supposed to teach them to lead worship?" The answer was obvious — "Show them."

I was not overly comfortable the first Sunday I left my guitar at home and led worship using only a microphone (and a few hand signals). I was very self-conscious and even, to some extent, inhibited. I knew that I was very dependent upon (and very vulnerable to) the other musicians. I made it through that Sunday and soon became rather adept at leading without my guitar. In doing so, I was able to show others that it was not just possible to muddle through, but to be very effective at leading even without playing a musical instrument. It wasn't comfortable for me, but it was necessary.

If we simply stay where we are comfortable, we will probably never grow or cause others to grow. We have a need to stretch ourselves and thereby cause growth.

Even as I write, the worship team I lead has temporarily lost our main piano player due to a new baby in her household. To help us through this phase we added a new keyboardist to our worship team. She is an extremely gifted high school student. However, when our former piano player returns the "new kid" will not pack up and leave. She will remain with us learning more about playing our keyboard-synthesizer. She will, in fact, be taking over much of the synthesizer playing from one of our "seasoned veterans." Will the veteran keyboardist be leaving the team? No, she will be working with the new girl to help her be effective in that role. This will probably not be as comfortable as simply playing the synthesizer herself, but comfort must not be our major aim.

Jesus clearly told us that we are to "Go therefore and *make disciples* of all the nations" (Matthew 28:19). He did not tell us to do it if we felt comfortable doing it. He just told us to do it.

I have learned from having a young son how God must feel toward us sometimes. Regardless of what I am doing, my son wants to help. It is usually much easier for me to do the work myself, but if I do not let him help, he will never learn. I must teach him, even when it is easier not to. Certainly God feels the same way toward us at times.

Ephesians 4:12 tells us that the role of leadership in the church is to equip the rest of the people for the work of the ministry. Sometimes it is easier for us to simply do it ourselves, but that is not God's best. I would have been more comfortable continuing to lead with my guitar and never showing the others that it is possible to lead without it, but then they (and I) would have missed God's plan. We cannot do just what is comfortable. We must do what the Lord asks. ❖

Chapter 24

Preparing to Lead

A number of years ago I had the privilege of attending a worship conference where Judson Cornwall was the main speaker. During one of the evening sessions he read from Revelation 7:9, "...I looked, and behold, a great multi- tude... from every nation... standing before the throne... clothed in white robes..." He stopped reading there and made this statement: "The more that I travel and get to know God and His people, the more I am convinced of the absolute necessity of vestments in worship." Everyone in the auditorium must have had the same quizzical look on their faces as I did because Dr. Cornwall caught himself and said, "Oh wait a minute... we're not on the same wavelength. I'm not talking about the physical. You can come before the Lord in blue jeans and bare feet if you like. That's between you and Him. I'm talking about the spiritual: the only way we can come before the Lord is clothed in the white robes which Jesus purchased for us at Calvary."

Some people say that praise is the door to the presence of the Lord. I understand the underlying meaning of their statement, and yet this view falls short of what the Bible teaches. "I am the way, and the truth, and the life; *no one comes to the Father, but through Me*" (John 14:6). "...we have confidence to enter the holy place *by the blood of Jesus*..." (Hebrews 10:19). The only way we can come before the Father is by the blood which Jesus shed on the cross. Singing is not the door, Jesus is.

In practical terms we need to appropriate those white robes for ourselves before we attempt to worship. We must realize anew each time that it is only by His grace and mercy that we can come before His presence. In and of ourselves we are not worthy but He, by His own blood, has made us worthy.

Have you ever come rushing in to a service at the last minute and tried to worship the Lord? It is usually difficult at best. We need to take time to prepare our hearts, to receive His forgiveness, to be ready to worship.

This preparation is different for each person. Our worship team meets at the church 45 minutes before the first Sunday morning service. I have instructed them to arrive ready, not just to sing and play music, but to worship the Lord. For some team members, the preparation time is in the car on the way to the church. Others may need to take more time at home or at the church. I arrive over an hour before the rest of the team. This gives me plenty of time to prepare my heart. Whatever heart preparation you require, take the time needed to be ready to worship.

Beyond heart preparation is the physical preparation. It is amazing to me how rampant the lack of preparation is within the charismatic movement. The church overall associates being spontaneous with being led by the Holy Spirit. Planning or preparation is usually associated with being in the flesh or, at least, not being led by the Spirit. Nowhere does the Bible teach this. As a matter of fact the opposite is true. God Himself had a plan for salvation since before time began. It was not a last minute, spontaneous thought; it was carefully planned out. God's Word promises that if we commit our works to the Lord that our "plans will be established" (Proverbs 16:3). Even Luke, the gospel writer, was a planner. He did careful research (Luke 1:1-3) before writing his account of Jesus' life. Was he led by the Holy Spirit in this research? II Timothy 3:16 says that he was.

It is not wrong to plan. In fact, it is very much within the will of the Lord to be prepared. It only becomes wrong when our planning precludes the leading of the Spirit of God. I often half-jokingly say that I am sure the Lord knows what He wants to happen on Sunday morning at least by Saturday night. If you ask Him to clue you in on what your part is to be, you at least give Him opportunity to give you any direction He wants you to have in order to rightly lead His people in worship.

I am frequently amazed at how natural the leading of the Lord can be. A number of years ago I heard another worship leader make a statement which really struck home with me. The statement was this: "As a worship leader I am not just given to myself; I am given to God and His people." This means that very often the thoughts that I have, the things going on in my life, the songs I find myself singing throughout the week are not just for me; they are for God's people as well. If I really understand this it makes a big difference in my preparation. It allows me to truly rely on the leading of the Holy Spirit. I do not need to wonder whether He is really leading me, I know He is. In John 10:27, Jesus tells us that, "My sheep hear My voice..." You are His sheep and you *do* hear His voice. Understanding and believing this truth makes preparing to lead worship much easier.

After careful, prayerful planning I am still open to those spontaneous promptings during the service. However, I have found that if I am truly open to His leading ahead of time, a major change during the service is the exception rather than the rule. The Lord has promised to lead His church. He did not say it would just be on the spur of the moment. He can even lead us in advance. ❖

Chapter 25

Understanding the Dynamics of the Worship Service

F inally we get to what everyone thinks about when they discuss worship leaders. I have purposely devoted only one chapter of this book to the actual service. The art of leading worship could be an entire book by itself. However, it is essential for us to understand that the service itself is important, but any service will only be as successful as the foundations you have laid for it.

It is always fascinating for me to watch an athletic contest like the International Olympics. Some of the events are over in just a few minutes (some even a matter of seconds), and that is all that we see. We get to view the climax but not the things leading up to that climax. We see the person (or people) win the big event, usually without much difficulty. We miss the years of training which preceded the win. In the same way, most people see only the actual service. They get blessed and assume that this is all there is to being a worship leader. Like Olympic viewers, they miss the important training and preparation involved. Still, without the training, the groundwork, the preparation, no medals are won, no victories complete, no glory gained. Inversely, if *you* lay the proper groundwork your actual times of leading worship will be far more effective. As a result, souls may be won, victories gained and glory given to the Author of praise.

Once you have prepared for a specific service (previous chapter) then you are ready to lead. It is important to note that although you have done the necessary homework, it is still absolutely imperative that you remain open and attentive to the Holy Spirit *while you lead*.

I mentioned earlier that a major change in plans is unusual if you have prepared properly. Notice that I never said that it is impossible. For some reason, we generally seem to be more "tuned in" during the service than at any other time. This may be due in part to the urgency of the moment. After all, we are now "in the spotlight" instead of just getting ready. Whatever the reason, I almost always encounter at least minute variations from what I plan. Sometimes these variations are even quite extreme. We should realize ahead of time that variance is a possibility and not be thrown totally off balance if it happens.

Perhaps a prophetic word will come forth that dramatically changes the flow of the service. If you (and possibly other leadership) judge that it is the word of the Lord for that moment then your song list may well be preempted. Be open to such a possibility.

Here are a few other helpful tips to use during the service:

Creating a Flow

It is helpful to create a "flow" during the service. Jumping back and forth between different types of songs (fast, slow, fast, slow) or even continually stopping and starting can be very disruptive to the worshippers. Use medleys of songs, flowing from one right into another. This continuity will create a comfortable atmosphere which allows the participants to focus in on the Lord instead of wondering what is going to happen next.

Using "Open Worship" Chord Progressions

Use simple chord progressions to allow the people to sing spontaneously unto the Lord. These times are referred to as "open worship," "free worship," or "singing in the Spirit with more than one chord." Whatever terminology you use, these times allow more freedom for the worshippers to express their own heart-felt worship unto God. These can be basic two chord progressions, more complex progressions using several chords, or even the last line of many songs works well for this.

Avoid Progressing Too Quickly

I am sometimes frustrated by people's lack of response to worship, especially at the beginning of the service. Then I realize that I have spent much time in prayer and preparation for the service. Many of them have spent no time in preparation (this is not an excuse for them, but it is a fact) and they are not mentally, physically or spiritually prepared to enter the presence of the Lord. If I decide to forge on ahead I may leave many of them behind. I must allow them to progress ahead with me and be careful not to leave them in the dust.

One concept I have found beneficial in this area is repeating songs, especially shorter ones, a few times. This allows the truth of the words to penetrate the minds and hearts of the people more thoroughly than just singing a song one time through. Try to find a balance between repeating a song enough times to allow it to "sink in" and moving on before the song becomes overly repetitious.

Keep Your Eyes on the Lord

This is probably the best advice for any and all situations, but especially problem situations. When the microphone fails to work, when you break a guitar string, when things are not going quite as planned, keep your eyes on the Lord. Always remember that you are not there to impress people or to show off your talents; your job is to lead people before the throne of God. Keeping your eyes on Him will make it easier for people to follow. In this area, your preparation time will be extremely beneficial. You will be less likely to become flustered or distracted if you have sought the mind of the Lord ahead of time. Keeping your focus on God will be much easier if, because of preparation, you can be less conscious of the music and the details of what is going on and more conscious of God Himself and what the Holy Spirit desires to do in the hearts of the people. ❖

Chapter 26

Desiring and Pursuing Excellence

I just visited a fascinating new exhibit at the St. Louis Zoo. In it there are numerous displays of "exotic" animals from around the world. Unfortunately, all through the exhibit there are blatant as well as subtle inferences to evolution. As I walked through the display two feelings came over me. The first was pity for the learned scientists who believe that all of these things came into being simply by chance. The second was an overwhelming awe of the God of creation Who made all of these creatures. His creativity is limitless. The variety in those creatures was so great that it seems to take more "faith" to believe that they were an accident than to believe in a God Who created them.

God apparently held nothing back when He created the earth on which we live. Why, after all, did the Lord make the creatures in the ocean depths which no human would even discover until this century? Why did He make each animal unique? And why so many different kinds? Would not just a few dozen have been sufficient? It seems apparent that God chose to make creation not just a half-hearted effort but the absolute best it could be. This attitude was manifest in Jesus also. When the people witnessed His healing ministry they responded, "He has done all things well..." (Mark 7:37).

We in the church need to grasp the concept of excellence more fully, especially in the music department. Too often I hear things like, "Well, it's good enough for church" or "The congregation will be singing along so they won't notice our mistakes." This attitude is totally opposite from God's attitude.

If we really want to follow the Lord, then we have no choice but to desire and pursue excellence. The standard of excellence is simply a part of the nature of the God Whom we serve. We need to strike the death blow to mediocrity within the church. If we can grasp and implement this attitude in our ministries, I believe we will see the blessing of God poured out upon us to maintain it.

Praying toward that end is the main key. Throughout Scripture God repeatedly caused His people to stand out from the crowd. "And as for these four youths, God gave them knowledge and intelligence in every branch of literature and wisdom; Daniel even understood all kinds of visions and dreams... And as for every matter of wisdom and understanding about which the king consulted them, he found them ten times better than all the magicians and conjurers who were in all his realm" (Daniel 1:17, 20). God is no respecter of persons. What He did for Shadrach, Meshach, Abed-nego and Daniel, He can do for us if we will ask Him.

We should realize that although our society may disagree, there are some absolutes in life. We have been taught that everything is relative. There are, however, certain standards which we can and should uphold regardless of the opinion of others. Striving for excellence in all that we do is one of these. It is not just a good idea, it is an absolute.

It has been said that excellence speaks a language all its own. We must pursue excellence with all our might.

One key point here is how we measure excellence. God's Word is the final true measuring rod. Walking in grace, however, we need to be careful not to compare ourselves with other people and/or other people's ideas. "But let each one examine his own work, and then he will have reason for boasting in regard to himself alone, and not in regard to another" (Galatians 6:4). If we are stretching ourselves to strive for *more* excellence we are headed in the right direction.

In reality, all of the things we have discussed prior to this chapter are a part of pursuing excellence. Maintaining your relationship with God, caring for people, getting organized and ministering beyond where you are comfortable — all of these are steps in the pursuit of excellence. But beyond the individual steps there is a heart attitude that says, "Regardless of what others think, regardless of what it costs me, I will pursue Godly excellence, even as my Creator has pursued it."

If we will pursue this attitude of excellence in all that we do, God will be honored and, in return, honor our efforts. Continue to seek the Lord and ask Him for His creativity in pursuing excellence in all that you do. He will not fail you. ❖

Epilogue

Well, if you made it this far, I hope you have learned a few things along the way. You now know the sum total of all that I have learned about being an effective worship leader. (Okay, maybe there are a few things I have held back for future writings...) So what else can I say at this point to stir you on in your walk with and service to Him? Just this: I have the utmost honor and respect for you as a child of the

King. Without question, if you are a worship leader, you are fulfilling one of the most challenging, difficult and yet spiritually rewarding roles in the church today. As a "front line warrior" you can have a powerful, long-term impact upon the people which God allows you to lead. Do not ever belittle the calling or the gift which the Lord has given you. Your ministry *will* have the effect He has ordained for it. "For I am confident of this very thing, that He who began a good work in you will perfect it until the day of Christ Jesus" (Philippians 1:6). May the Lord continue to lead you on from strength to strength until His return. Amen. ❖

Appendix

New Song Sources

- **Christ for the Nations Institute**
Box 769000, Dallas, TX 75376-9000

- **Integrity's Hosanna! Music**
P.O. Box 16801, Mobile, AL 36616
(205) 633-9000

- **Maranatha! Music**
30230 Rancho Viejo Road
San Juan Capistrano, CA 92675
(714) 248-4000

- **People of Destiny Music**
7881-B Beechcraft, Gaithersburg, MD 20879
(301) 948-4890

- **Scripture in Song**
P.O. Box 525, Lewiston, NY 14092

- **Vineyard Music**
P.O. Box 65004, Anaheim, CA 92815
(714) 533-9281

Other Books by Tom Kraeuter

Keys to Becoming an Effective Worship Leader

This book has sold over 30,000 copies and continues to be the standard for worship leaders world-wide.

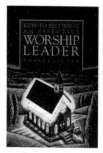

Bill Rayborn of The Church Music Report said this: "In very practical, down-to-earth terms Tom leads you through a journey into the heart of the effective worship leader... a journey needed by us all!"

Developing an Effective Worship Ministry

This is the A - Z book on developing the ministry of praise and worship in the local church. Worship team guidelines, establishing a vision for music ministry, finding the right people, the pastor's role in the worship ministry, etc.

Things They Didn't Teach Me In Worship Leading School

The experiences of 50 prominent worship leaders from around the world packed into one encouraging and insightful book. Includes stories from Graham Kendrick, LaMar Boschman, Bob Fitts, Steve Fry, and many more.

Worship Is... What?!

Rethinking Our Ideas About Worship

In his usual story-filled way, Tom makes the Scriptures come alive for today. If you want to understand what worship is all about — or if you think you already do — you should read this book.

The Worship Leader's Handbook

Practical question-and-answer format makes this no-holds-barred book a must-have for every worship leader. Arranged in topical sections for easy use. You'll refer to it again and again. You'll wonder how you got along without it!

ORDER FORM

	QTY	EACH	TOTAL
Worship Is...What?!		$ 8.00	
If Standing Together Is So Great, Why Do We Keep Falling Apart?		$ 9.00	
Things They Didn't Teach Me in Worship Leading School		$10.00	
Keys to Becoming an Effective Worship Leader		$ 9.00	
Developing an Effective Worship Ministry		$ 9.00	
The Worship Leader's Handbook		$ 9.00	
			·
		Subtotal	
Postage/Packaging — 10% of subtotal for U.S. & Canada, minimum $3.00; 40% for overseas			
		TOTAL	

PAYMENT OPTIONS

☐ Enclosed is my check for $_____

☐ Credit Card — Please bill my:

☐ MC ☐ Visa Credit Card Exp._____

Card#_____

Signature_____

Name_____

_____

Address_____

City_____ST_____ZIP_____

Phone_____E-mail_____

FOR ORDERS: **Call:** 1-800-922-2143
Or Write to: Emerald Books
PO Box 635
Lynnwood, WA 98046

VERSION A